21st Century Skills **INNOVATION LIBRARY**

MINDST

Level 2

CHERRY LAKE PUBLISHING • **ANN ARBOR, MICHIGAN**

by Rena Hixon

CHERRY LAKE Publishing

A Note to Adults: Please review the instructions for the activities in this book before allowing children to do them. Be sure to help them with any activities you do not think they can safely complete on their own.

A Note to Kids: Be sure to ask an adult for help with these activities when you need it. Always put your safety first!

Published in the United States of America by Cherry Lake Publishing
Ann Arbor, Michigan
www.cherrylakepublishing.com

Reading Adviser: Marla Conn, Read With Me Now
Photo Credits: Cover and page 1, ©PRNewsFoto/The LEGO Group; pages 4, 6, 11, 12, 13, 15 ,16 ,19, 21, 24, 26, 27, and 28, Rena Hixon; page 8, ©Tiramisu Studio/Shutterstock

Library of Congress Cataloging-in-Publication Data
Hixon, Rena, author.
  Mindstorms. Level 2 / by Rena Hixon.
    pages cm.—(21st century skills innovation library. Unofficial guides)
  Audience: Grades 4 to 6.
  Includes bibliographical references and index.
  ISBN 978-1-63470-525-7 (lib. bdg.)—ISBN 978-1-63470-645-2 (pbk.)—
ISBN 978-1-63470-585-1 (pdf)—ISBN 978-1-63470-705-3 (ebook)
1. LEGO Mindstorms toys—Juvenile literature. 2. Robotics—Juvenile literature.
3. Detectors—Juvenile literature. 4. Computer programming—Juvenile literature.
I. Title.
  TJ211.2.H485 2016
  629.8'92—dc23   2015030340

Cherry Lake Publishing would like to acknowledge the work of The Partnership for 21st Century Skills. Please visit *www.p21.org* for more information.

Printed in the United States of America
Corporate Graphics
January 2016

Contents

Chapter 1	**The Sonar Sensor**	**4**
Chapter 2	**The Infrared Sensor**	**12**
Chapter 3	**The Color Sensor**	**17**
Chapter 4	**The Touch Sensor**	**25**
	Glossary	**30**
	Find Out More	**31**
	Index	**32**
	About the Author	**32**

Chapter 1

The Sonar Sensor

f you're reading this book, you probably already know about some of the incredible things you can do with Lego Mindstorms. You may even have built some Mindstorms robots yourself. Hopefully you know what the different parts do, how to make a basic program, and how to use the EV3 programmable brick. If not, you should start by reading *Unofficial Guides: Mindstorms Level 1*. Then come back to this book once you're ready!

Adding sensors to your projects will greatly expand what you can do with Mindstorms.

The focus of this book will be learning how to use **sensors** in your Mindstorms projects. Sensors collect information about their environment. They send this information to the EV3 programmable brick. The EV3 responds to the information in different ways depending on how it is programmed. For example, you might create a program that allows a robot to detect and avoid obstacles.

There are two different Mindstorms EV3 kits available for purchase. The retail kit comes with a color sensor and a touch sensor. The education kit has those sensors, too. However, it also includes an **ultrasonic** sensor and a **gyro** sensor. The retail kit has an **infrared** sensor and a remote control that can be used with it.

This book covers the color sensor, touch sensor, ultrasonic sensor, and infrared sensor. The gyro sensor is more complex than the others. If you want to learn more about it, check out the other books in this series.

Let's start by learning how to use the ultrasonic sensor. This is the one that looks like it has round red eyes. It is commonly referred to as the **sonar** sensor.

This is because it works a lot like the sonar ability used by bats. A bat can send out special sound waves. You can't hear them, but they bounce off nearby objects and return to the bat. The bat then knows how far away different objects are, how fast they are moving, and which direction they are heading in. The Mindstorms sonar sensor uses a similar technique to determine the distance of objects.

The sonar sensor has two round, red "eyes."

You can learn a little about the sonar sensor before you use it to build a robot. Attach a sonar sensor to one of the four **input ports** on the EV3. The input ports are labeled 1, 2, 3, and 4. It doesn't matter which one you use right now.

On the EV3, select the **icon** with six small circles, then choose the "Port View" option. Now choose the port number of the attached sonar sensor. You should see the readings of the sensor measured in centimeters. Pick up the sonar sensor and move it around. See what types of readings you get. You should notice that the number goes up the farther the sensor is from an object. Moving the sensor closer should make the number go down. Try to get the number as high and low as possible. In theory, the lowest number that you should be able to read is 0. However, you will find that it is very difficult to get a reading of 0. The smallest you can detect will likely be around 4 centimeters. The largest reading you can get is 255 centimeters.

The EV3 can also display sensor readings in inches. To try this out, hit the middle button on the EV3 while still viewing the port. It will display three options: "US-DIST-CM", "US-DIST-IN", and "US-Listen". Select "US-DIST-IN". Check the minimum and maximum values that you can read in inches. Again, you should

Sensors All Around

Sensors like the ones used in Mindstorms projects are all around you. These devices are common parts of many everyday devices. Have you ever used a touchless sink or hand dryer in a public bathroom? These devices use sensors to detect when your hands are near.

Another place you might find sensors is on your family car. It is common for newer vehicles to include sensors that detect cars or other objects around them. They then alert the driver so he or she can react to avoid an accident.

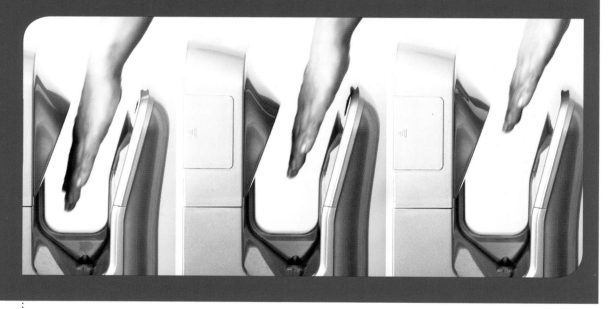

be able to get a reading of 0 in theory, but you will find it difficult to get anything lower than about 1.2 inches. The maximum reading is 100.3 inches.

It is time to build a robot and see what you can do with the sonar sensor! You can find directions for building a simple robot at *www.damienkee.com/home/2013/8/2/rileyrover-ev3-classroom-robot-design.html.* Follow these instructions and attach the sonar sensor.

Now you are going to program a robot to avoid objects. Open the Lego Mindstorms EV3 software and start a new program. When your sonar sensor detects an object, you want your robot to turn away from it. Then you want it to keep doing this over and over again, until you get tired of watching it and turn it off!

In order to make a robot do something over and over again, you need to create something called a loop. You will find the "Loop" icon under the light-orange button. Bring that into your program. The **default** is for an unlimited loop. This means the loop will never end until you turn off the robot.

The next icon you need is "Move Tank". Add it to your program and place it inside the loop. Set it to turn on motors B and C. Do not specify a distance on your motors. You want them to stay on until the sonar sensor detects an object. So the next icon you are going to use is "Wait". This icon is also under the light-orange button. Once you've added it to your loop, you have to tell it what to wait for. Choose "Ultrasonic Sensor" and select "Compare Inches". Don't forget to select the port your sonar sensor is plugged into.

You can program the EV3 to check for measurements that are *equal to*, *not equal to*, *less than*, *less than or equal to*, *greater than*, or *greater than or equal to*. You can choose *less than* or *less than or equal to* for this experiment. The distance is under the rectangle icon with a red dot. The smaller the number you choose, the closer your robot will get to an object before turning. As you discovered earlier, you should not use a number smaller than 4 centimeters or 1.2 inches.

The next thing you need to do is program your robot to turn when it gets too close to an object. It does not matter which direction it turns. Bring a "Move Tank" icon into your loop. Choose whichever settings you want. Think back to the activities in the previous book in this series. Do you remember how to make your robot turn at different speeds?

Below is an example of what a finished program should look like. The sonar sensor is attached to port 2, and the motors are attached to **output** ports B and C. Download the program to your EV3 and run it. Your robot should move forward and turn to avoid any objects in front of it. Try sending your robot through a maze. Then see if you can keep it from falling off a table.

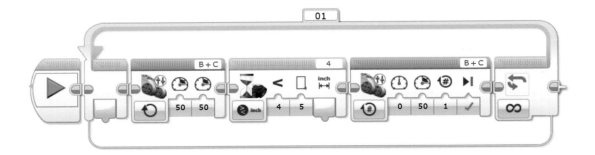

Chapter 2

The Infrared Sensor

Now that you know how to use the sonar sensor, let's try out the infrared sensor. Start by attaching the infrared sensor to a port. Select the "Port View" option just as you did with the sonar sensor. What do you notice about the values it displays? While the sonar sensor read in centimeters and inches, the infrared sensor measures distance

The infrared sensor looks somewhat like the sonar sensor, but with narrower "eyes."

from 0 to 100. A value of 0 means an object is very
close. A value of 100 means the object is far away.

Go back to the program you created in chapter 1.
You can replace the "Wait" for ultrasonic with a "Wait" for
infrared. Your robot should perform a lot like it did with
the sonar sensor. However, the sensor works differently
to accomplish its job. Remember that the sonar sensor
uses sound waves that you can't hear. Instead, the
infrared sensor uses light waves that you can't see. While
the infrared sensor can be used to measure distance like
the sonar sensor, it can also do other things.

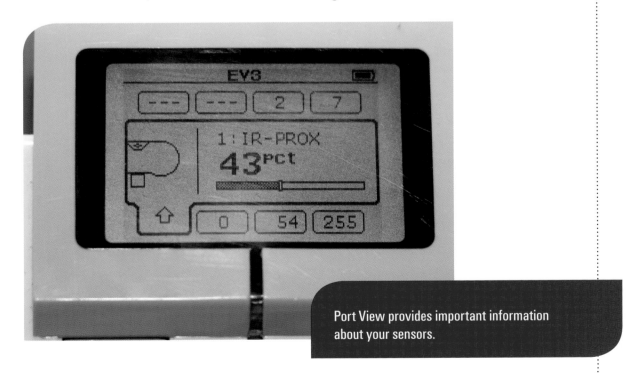

Port View provides important information about your sensors.

For example, the infrared sensor can be used along with a remote control. The Mindstorms remote has four different channels, numbered 1 through 4. Channel 1 is when the red switch is pushed up as far as it can go toward the black end of the remote. Channel 2 is the next position down, then 3, and then 4. The program determines which channel is used with your robot. If you use channel 3, another robot can use one of the other channels. This would allow you to switch between two robots using the same remote. If you put two robots with infrared sensors on the same channel, you can control them both at the same time. The program for each robot could tell it to do something different than the other one.

A program can be used to assign functions to each of the remote's buttons. Suppose you want to use the remote to control the motors on your robot. You could use one button to make the right motor go forward and another to make the motor go backward. You can also program more complicated controls. For example, you might program the motors to turn off when two buttons are pressed at once. Open up the EV3 software and see if you can figure out how to program some basic remote controls for the robot you built in chapter 1. Below is one possible solution. Remember to make sure the channel is set correctly in your program. It needs to match the channel you are using on your remote.

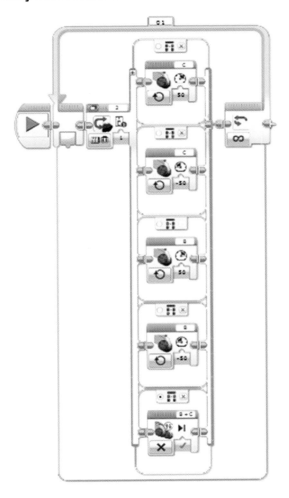

Incredible Infrared

You have probably used an infrared sensor before without knowing it. Most computer mice rely on infrared sensors to detect movement. The sensors send out infrared light from the bottom of the mouse. As a user moves the mouse across a surface, the sensors transmit information about its speed and position to the computer. This information moves the cursor around on the computer screen.

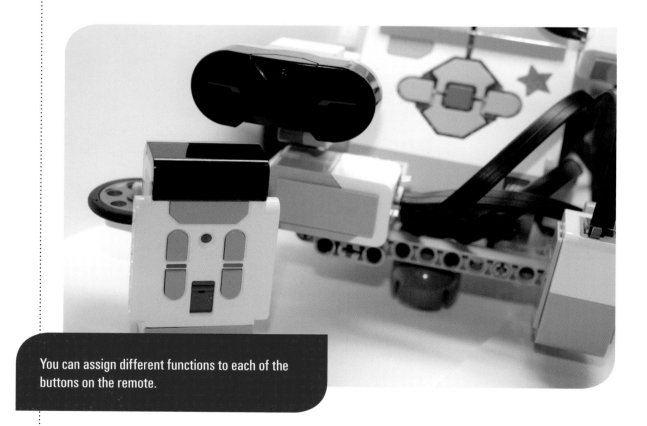

You can assign different functions to each of the buttons on the remote.

Chapter 3

The Color Sensor

N ext, let's try out the color sensor. This device has two main settings. It can be used to detect light, or it can be used to detect a certain color. When it is being used for color, this book will refer to it as a color sensor. When it is being used for light, it will be referred to as a light sensor. When using it as a light sensor, you will notice a red light on the device. If you use it as a color sensor, the light will be different.

Look at the light sensor before plugging it in. You will see two things that look like lightbulbs. One is quite a bit larger than the other one. Connect the sensor to the EV3 and select the "Port View" option. The default is for the sensor to measure reflected light. You should notice that the larger lightbulb is sending out a red light. This light reflects off of objects. The smaller bulb on the sensor reads this reflected light. The sensor can then determine how dark or light the object is.

Experiment with the light sensor. Try to figure out the maximum and minimum values that can be detected. Are dark colors lower values or higher values? What is the lowest value you can detect? What is the highest? You should find that dark colors reflect less light and give smaller values. You should have been able to detect 0 fairly easily. Light colors give larger values. If you found just the right object, you could read a value as high as 100. For example, you should hit 100 if you point the sensor at the EV3 unit from the right distance.

Press the middle button on the EV3 while in Port View. You will see three options: "COL-REFLECT", "COL-AMBIENT", and "COL-COLOR". Select "COL-COLOR". The sensor is now ready to detect color. Take a look at the sensor's larger bulb. You should notice that instead of sending out a red light, it now sends out different colors. Point the sensor at different colors of Lego pieces. You should notice that different colors cause the EV3 screen to display different numbers. A reading of 0 indicates that there is no color detected. Try to find out what colors relate to what numbers. How many did you find?

The color sensor's larger bulb emits light. The smaller one reads the light that is reflected back to the sensor.

The sensor can detect seven different colors:

0 = No Color

1 = Black

2 = Blue

3 = Green

4 = Yellow

5 = Red

6 = White

7 = Brown

Another light source you can experiment with is **ambient** light. Press the center button while in Port View, then select "COL-AMBIENT". In this mode, the light sensor is reading light in the room around it instead of light reflected from an object. The range of detectable values is 0 through 100 again. Move into darker and brighter rooms. You should see higher values in brighter areas and lower ones in darker areas.

Let's take a closer look at the reflected light readings. Set the sensor back to "COL-REFLECT". Lay the sensor flat on the surface of a black piece of paper and look at the reading on the EV3. Now try the same thing on a white piece of paper. It is probably going to be very close to the same value for both readings. Now try it again, but very slowly move your light sensor up from the surface of the paper. Pay attention to the readings as you go. You should notice that you get better differences between the white and black readings when the light sensor is about 0.25 to 0.5 inches (0.64 to 1.27 cm) away from the source. As the sensor gets farther away, it will detect less difference in the readings. Keeping this in mind, secure the sensor to the same robot you used in the previous chapters.

Now you are going to use the light sensor to keep your robot inside an oval shape. You will need a large piece of poster board and some black electrical tape. Use the electrical tape to make an oval on the poster board. Set your robot on the poster board. Check the values in Port View again. If they are not very different between the white poster board and black tape, you need to adjust the height of the sensor from the ground.

The program for this activity is going to be very similar to the programs you wrote to make your robot avoid objects. What do you think the main difference will be? Instead of programming the robot to wait for ultrasonic or infrared readings, you will program it to

Black tape on a white background is easiest for your sensor to read.

Let There Be Light

Have you ever been riding in a car in the evening and noticed the streetlights suddenly turn on? Unlike the lights in your home, streetlights aren't controlled by a simple switch. Instead, they use sensors to turn on and off automatically as needed. Once a light sensor detects when the natural light isn't bright enough to see, the streetlights turn on. When the light sensor notices that it is bright outside again the next morning, they turn off.

wait for dark readings. This is a little trickier than the previous programs. You have to find the exact dark value of the tape you used to make your oval. Use your sensor in Port View to do this. It is best to set your robot down just as it would be when running, in order to read the values. This will give you more accurate readings. Back in the EV3 software, set the value on the "Wait" icon to about five more than the value of the dark you detected.

Download the program to your robot and run it. How is it working? You might notice that the robot sometimes turns too quickly when it hits the black line. This could cause it to move outside of the oval. Adjust the values in your program if you need to.

By now you should have a feel for the values your program needs to detect the electrical tape. Let's try writing a program that makes your robot travel around the oval by following the tape with the light sensor.

Rather than following the tape itself, the robot will follow the line where the black tape meets the white poster board. Before creating your program, you need to choose which direction your robot is going to travel and which side of the line to follow. The side of the line you choose to follow will change the direction your robot turns. If the example program doesn't work, try placing the robot on the other side of the line.

To follow a line, you will need the light sensor to tell the EV3 whether it is detecting the black of the electrical tape or the white of the poster board. Then you need the EV3 to make sure the robot stays pointed along the edge of the black tape. If your robot detects black, it should turn toward the white. If it detects white, it should turn toward the black. This will cause your robot to jiggle back and forth as it travels.

Start your program with an unlimited loop. Place a "Switch" icon inside your loop. Select the light sensor and compare for less than a reflected light value. (You can use the same values from the previous oval activity.) Program the robot to turn left if true (check mark). Program it to turn right if false (x). An example of a working program is below. However, the light values and ports may be different from the ones you used.

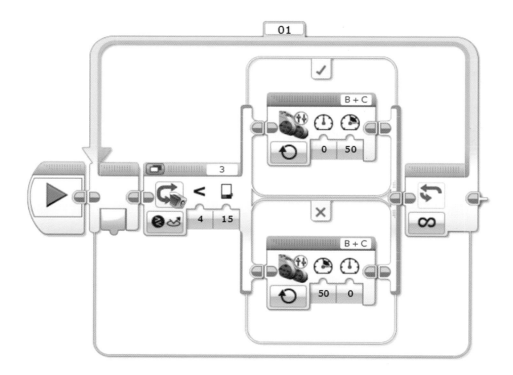

Download and run your program to see if it works. You should be able to test if your robot is working by holding it over the black line and checking to see if the stopped motor switches when it sees the line. If this is not happening, make sure the icons in your program are correct. You can also check to make sure your motors are connected correctly.

Once the program is working, try making a variety of paths for your robot to follow. Use the same colors of poster board and electrical tape to create different shapes. Your robot should be able to follow any of these paths!

Chapter 4

The Touch Sensor

The touch sensor is one of the simplest sensors in the EV3 kit. However, it has several important uses. Plug it in and access the Port View on the EV3. Play around with the sensor and keep an eye on the display. You might notice that there are only two possible values. If the sensor is pressed in, you will see a 1. If not, you will see a 0. That's it!

Let's write a program that makes your robot drive up to an object, touch the object, and stop. Start by mounting the sensor on the front of the robot. Can you write a program that will make your robot drive forward until the touch sensor is pressed? The first thing the program should do is turn on your motors. Now use a "Wait" icon and tell the robot to wait for a touch and turn off the motors.

Now let's try a program that makes your robot drive forward each time the touch sensor is bumped. What do you think the difference is between bumping and pressing the sensor? A bump waits for the touch sensor to be pressed and released before it performs an action. That means if you hold down the touch sensor, the EV3 will not do anything until you release it.

The touch sensor has a piece of red plastic that can be pushed inward.

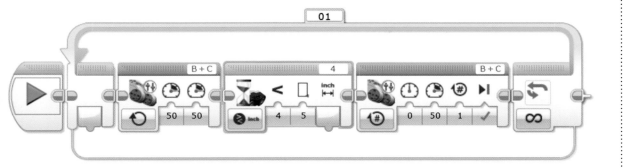

Start your program with a "Wait" icon that waits for the touch sensor. Select "Compare State".

Now add the "Move Tank" icon. Turn on motors B and C for degrees. Set the "Degrees" measurement to 90. Finally, put a loop around all of the **code**. Download and run your program. When you press and release the touch sensor, the robot should move forward slightly.

The last experiment is going to be to drive forward until the touch sensor is bumped and then change directions. Start with a loop. Then add a "Move Tank" icon. Just as in the previous program, tell the robot to wait until the touch sensor is bumped. Then use a "Move Tank" with negative numbers on the

What's Next?

Now that you know how to use the main sensors, you have a lot more options for creating your Mindstorms projects. What will you make next? Try building a remote-controlled car. Now try adding a sonar sensor and programming the car to stop moving anytime it gets close to a wall. You've created a remote-controlled car that can't crash! What other ways can you think of to combine the different sensors? Be creative, and don't worry if your ideas don't always work right away. Trying new things is the best way to improve your understanding of the Mindstorms system.

motors. This will make the robot go in reverse. Finally, tell the robot to wait until the touch sensor is bumped again. Download and run your program. Does it work like you planned? If you have any issues, check to make sure everything is connected correctly.

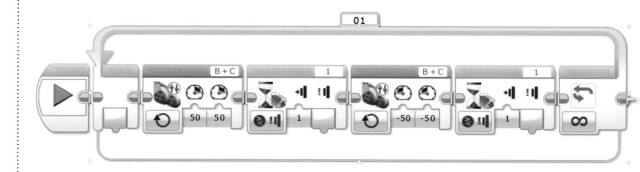

In this book, we have looked at the EV3's most commonly used sensors. Hopefully you are now comfortable avoiding objects with the sonar sensor, using the infrared sensor with a remote control, following a line with the light sensor, and detecting objects with the touch sensor. You should be able to use the programming language to control the robot using the information received from these sensors. Are you ready for the next steps?

Glossary

ambient (AM-bee-uhnt) relating to the immediate surroundings of an object

code (KODE) instructions for a computer written in a programming language

default (di-FAWLT) a setting or option that will be effective if you don't specifically choose one in a computer program

gyro (JYE-roh) a sensor that can determine direction, tilt, speed, and movement; short for *gyroscope*

icon (EYE-kahn) a graphic symbol on a computer screen that represents a program, function, or file

infrared (IN-fruh-red) a color of light that cannot be seen by the human eye

input (IN-put) information fed into a computer

output (OUT-put) information produced by a computer

ports (PORTS) places on a computer that are designed for a particular kind of plug

sensors (SEN-surz) devices that measure light, sound, movement, and touch

sonar (SOH-nar) an instrument that sends out sound waves to determine the location of objects

ultrasonic (uhl-truh-SAH-nik) sounds that are too high for a human ear to detect

Find Out More

BOOKS

Bagnall, Brian. *Maximum LEGO EV3: Building Robots with Java Brains.* Variant Press, 2014.

Garber, Gary. *Instant Lego Mindstorms EV3.* Birmingham, UK: Packt Publishing, 2013.

Griffin, Terry. *The Art of LEGO MINDSTORMS EV3 Programming.* San Francisco: No Starch Press, 2010.

WEB SITE

Lego Mindstorms: Build a Robot
www.lego.com/en-us/mindstorms/build-a-robot
Check out instructions for building other Mindstorms robots.

Index

channels, 14, 15
color sensor, 5, 17,
  18–19

distance readings, 6,
  7–8, 12–13

EV3 brick, 4, 5
EV3 software, 9,
  14–15, 22

gyro sensor, 5

infrared sensor, 5,
  12–16
input ports, 7, 10, 11

light sensor, 17–18,
  20–23
loops, 9–10, 23, 27

motors, 9, 11, 14, 24,
  25, 27–28
"Move Tank" icon, 9,
  10, 27–28

remote control, 5,
  14–15, 28

"Switch" icon, 23

touch sensor, 5, 25–28

ultrasonic sensor,
  5–11, 28

"Wait" icon, 10, 13,
  22, 25, 27

About the Author

Rena Hixon received a bachelor's degree in computer science from the University of Missouri–Rolla (now Missouri University of Science and Technology). She also earned a doctorate in electrical engineering from Wichita State University. She worked as a software design engineer for 11 years and has taught computer science classes at Wichita State for more than 13 years. In 2004, Rena and her husband started a Lego robotics club for homeschooled students. Its aim is to teach engineering principles, emphasizing math and science, to children. Rena has also taught her own Lego robotics camps for 12 years as well as camps at Missouri S&T for several years.

CHERRY LAKE PUBLISHING • ANN ARBOR, MICHIGAN   by Rena Hixon

MINDST
Level 3

21st Century Skills **INNOVATION LIBRARY**

A Note to Adults: Please review the instructions for the activities in this book before allowing children to do them. Be sure to help them with any activities you do not think they can safely complete on their own.

A Note to Kids: Be sure to ask an adult for help with these activities when you need it. Always put your safety first!

Published in the United States of America by Cherry Lake Publishing
Ann Arbor, Michigan
www.cherrylakepublishing.com

Reading Adviser: Marla Conn, Read With Me Now
Photo Credits: Cover and page 1, ©AP Images; page 5, ©Robert Mandel/ Shutterstock; pages 17, 20, and 24, Rena Hixon; page 22, ©Beloborod/ Shutterstock; page 29, Érre/tinyurl.com/oa4efw6/CC BY-SA 2.0

Library of Congress Cataloging-in-Publication Data
Names: Hixon, Rena, author.
Title: Mindstorms. Level 3 / by Rena Hixon.
Description: Ann Arbor, Michigan : Cherry Lake Publishing, [2016] |
  Series: 21st century skills innovation library. Unofficial guides |
  Audience: Grades 4 to 6.- | Includes bibliographical references and index.
Identifiers: LCCN 2015034877| ISBN 9781634705264 (lib. bdg.) |
  ISBN 9781634706469 (pbk.) | ISBN 9781634705868 (pdf) |
  ISBN 9781634707060 (ebook)
Subjects: LCSH: LEGO Mindstorms toys–Juvenile literature. | Robotics–Juvenile
  literature. | Computer programming–Juvenile literature. | Detectors–Juvenile
  literature.
Classification: LCC TJ211.2 .H486 2016 | DDC 629.8/92–dc23 LC record
available at http://lccn.loc.gov/2015034877

Cherry Lake Publishing would like to acknowledge the work of The Partnership for 21st Century Skills. Please visit www.p21.org for more information.

Printed in the United States of America
Corporate Graphics
January 2016

Contents

Chapter 1 **Understanding Programming Concepts** **4**

Chapter 2 **Reading the Light Sensor** **12**

Chapter 3 **Checking a Range** **20**

Chapter 4 **Detecting and Counting Lines** **25**

Glossary **30**

Find Out More **31**

Index **32**

About the Author **32**

Chapter 1

Understanding Programming Concepts

I f you're reading this book, you probably already know about some of the incredible things you can do with Lego Mindstorms. You may have even built some Mindstorms robots yourself. Hopefully you know how the different sensors are used, how to create simple programs, and how to use the EV3 programmable brick. If not, you should start by reading *Unofficial Guides: Mindstorms Level 1* and *Level 2*. Then come back to this book once you're ready!

The EV3 software is extremely powerful. It can be used to create robots far more complex than the ones we made in previous books. This book will focus on creating programs that will allow your robots to do more than one thing at a time. For example, in the previous books, we made a robot that could follow a line and a robot that would stop before running into walls. But we can also write a program that tells a

robot how to do both of those things. In addition, we will look at some **icons** in the EV3 software that you can use to accomplish some more complex things with your robot.

Let's start by reviewing the basics of Mindstorms programming. We will use the same robot we built for the activities in Level 1 and Level 2.

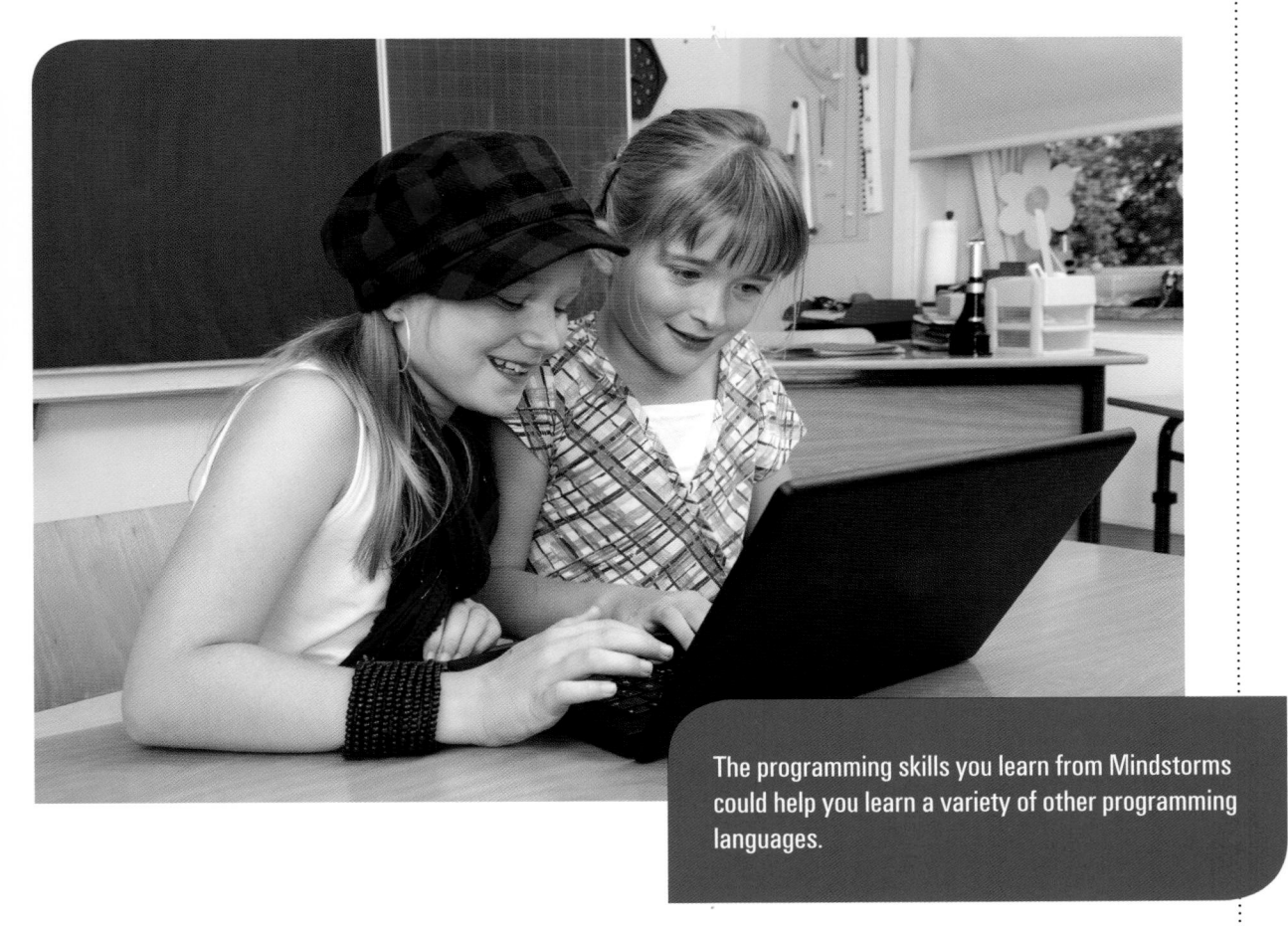

The programming skills you learn from Mindstorms could help you learn a variety of other programming languages.

In the EV3 software, drag the "Move Tank" icon into a new program. Set it to simply turn the motors on. For now, this will be the only icon in your program. Predict what you think will happen when you run it. Now give it a try. You might have predicted that the motors will run forever. However, either the robot will twitch slightly or nothing will happen at all! To understand why this is, you need to get familiar with some of the common EV3 icons. The green arrow icon is the "Start" icon. This is where every program will start. If you put icons in the programming screen that are not attached to the "Start" icon, nothing will happen.

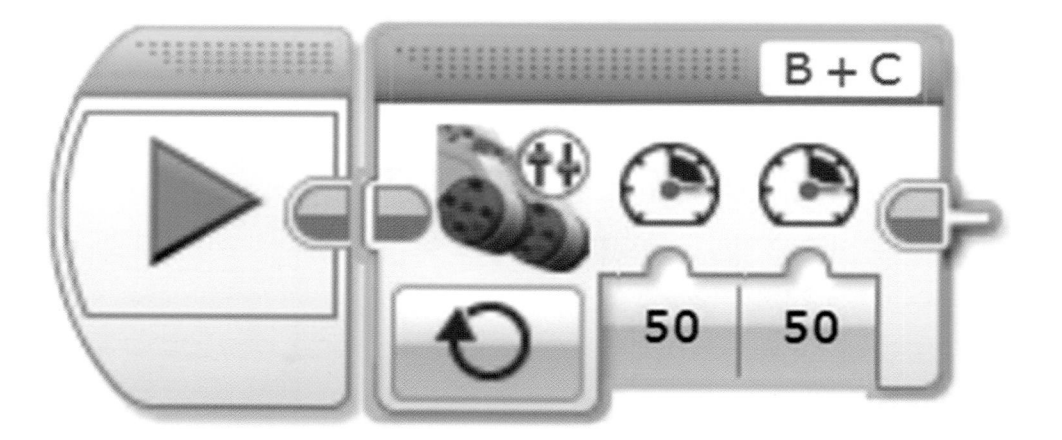

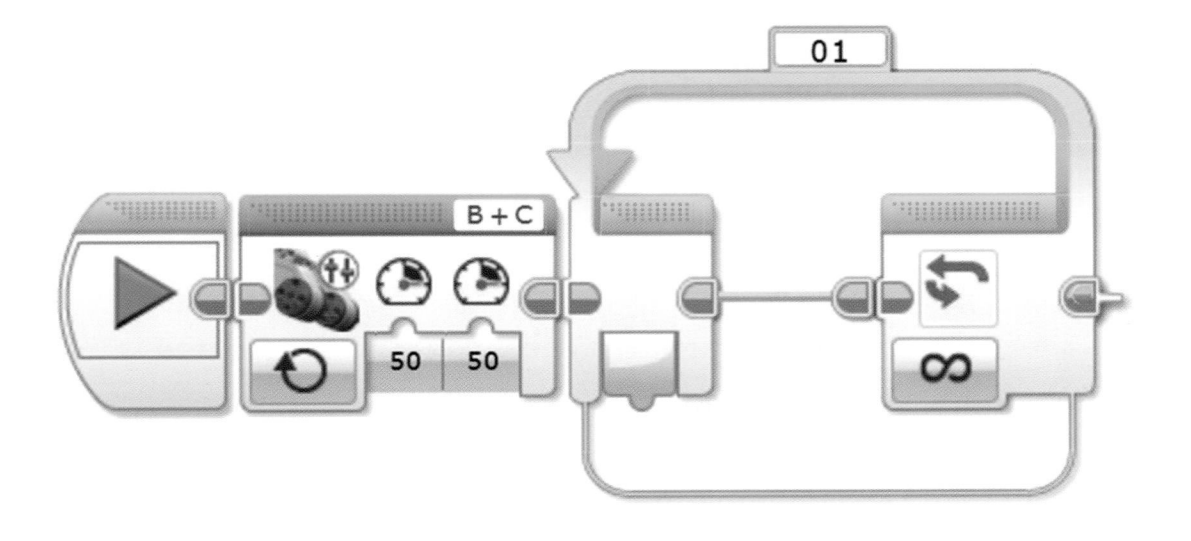

If you want the robot to actually turn on and run forever, then you should add a "Forever" loop to the end of the program. You might think you should put the "Move Tank" icon inside the loop. However, it is more accurate to put the loop after the icon. This way, you are turning on the motors and then telling the program to run forever. If the icon is inside the loop, then you are actually telling it to keep turning on the motors. Understanding these small differences is an important part of figuring out which order your icons should go in.

Another important concept to understand is that icons are executed in the order you see them on-screen. Therefore, if you want your robot to go forward and then make a turn, your icons should be placed in that order.

Another thing you need to understand about programming is that each icon is only **executed** once unless you use a loop to tell it otherwise. For example, many students are confused by the "Switch" icon. This icon checks a condition and then executes one of two actions based on the results. Most students assume that it will keep checking the condition and executing the right action. However, it will only check once unless a loop is around it.

In the following program, the "Switch" icon will be executed once. If it notices that the touch sensor is pressed, the robot will move forward one rotation. If the program is executed and the touch sensor is not pressed, the robot will go backward one rotation. Try running this program to make sure you under-stand the concept of a "Switch" icon only being executed one time.

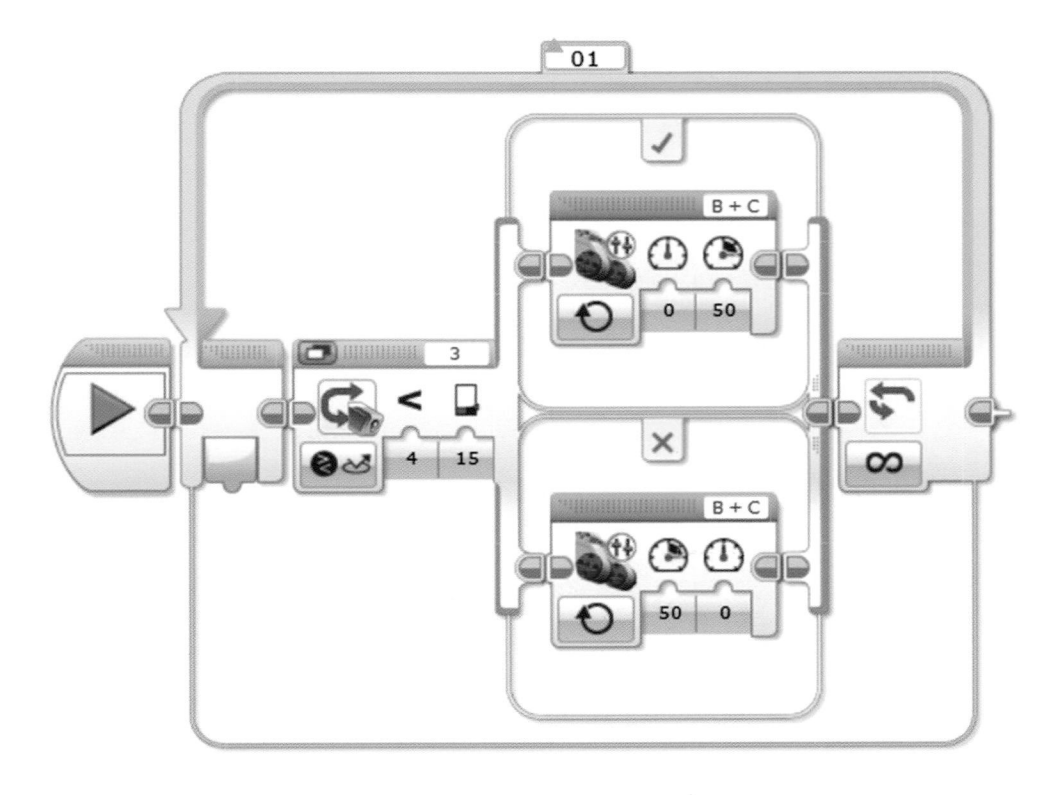

Look back to the line-following program we created in Level 2. This is a good example of a "Switch" icon that needs to execute more than once. The entire program must have a loop around it to keep checking the light value and steering the robot in the right direction. Without this loop, the robot would check the value once and stop.

If you have a loop in your program that has the infinity sign, it will loop forever. You should not expect your program to ever go past that loop.

All About Firmware

Like many electronic devices, the EV3 brick has special built-in software called firmware. Firmware is what allows your programs to run. It also tells the brick how to display information on the screen, how to communicate with sensors, and more. Sometimes the Lego company releases new versions of the EV3 firmware. These versions can add new features and improve the way the EV3 works. You can download them from the Internet and transfer them to your programmable brick much as you do with the programs you create in the EV3 software.

In order to continue your program, you need to get out of the loop.

Let's create a program that instructs our robot to follow a line until it detects an object within 4 inches (10.2 centimeters) in front of it. The robot should stop once it notices the object. Can you figure out how to write a program to accomplish this? In order to try it out, you can use the oval track we created for Level 2. Then set a box or some other object somewhere on top of the line.

Start by making a line-following program like the one in Level 2, then put a loop around it. However, don't use an infinite loop. The loop should only repeat until the ultrasonic sensor notices something less than 4 inches (10.2 cm) away. The last icon in

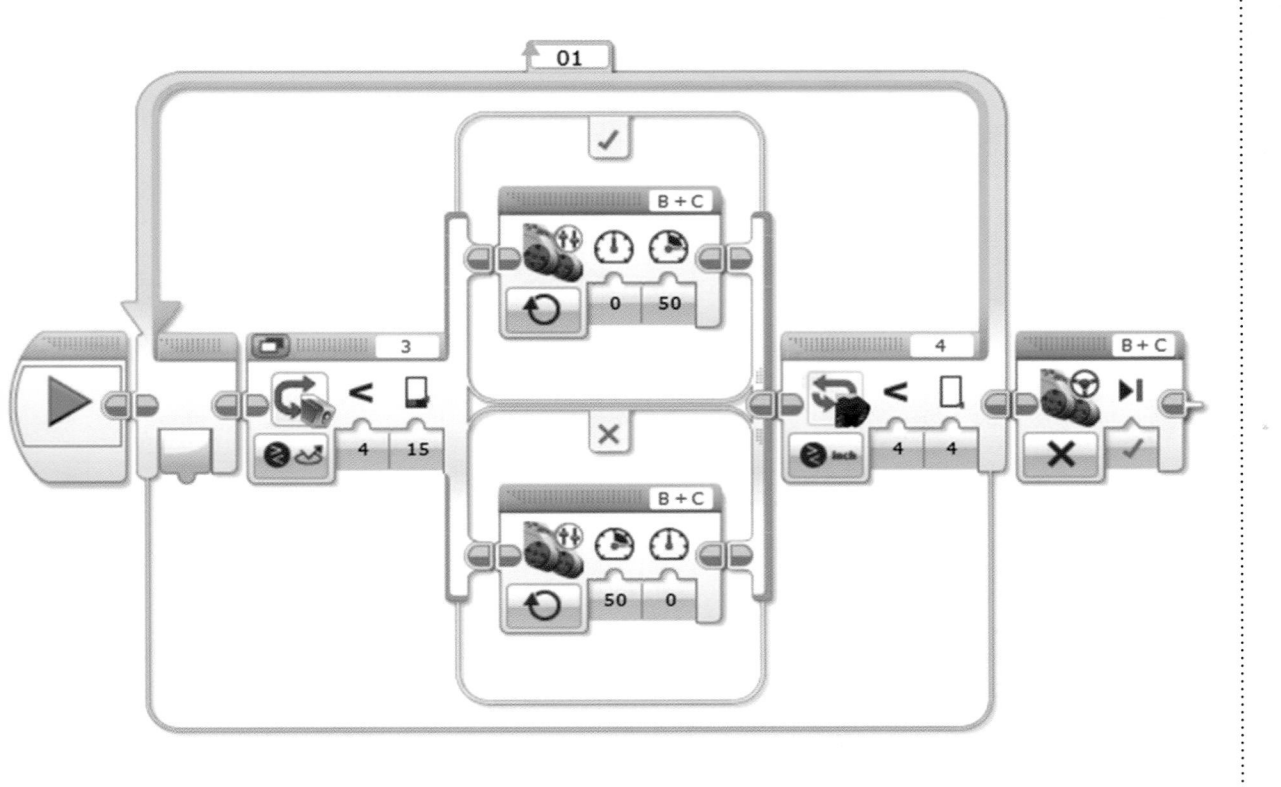

your program should be a "Move Tank" with the
motors turned off. For this program to work, you
need to have your ultrasonic sensor on the front of
your robot.

You are now ready to develop a course of your own
and figure out how to put together different program
parts to do several tasks. Use tape and poster board to
create a long course just like you did for the oval. Add
in plenty of curves and turns and obstacles.

Chapter 2

Reading the Light Sensor

As you keep working on more advanced Mindstorms projects, you are bound to run into difficulties from time to time. Luckily, there are some tricks you can use to help **troubleshoot** problems with your programs. The first thing you are going to learn in this chapter is how to display readings from the sensors on the EV3 screen. If you are having problems with a line-following program, for example, you might want to display the values that your robot is reading as it runs the program.

To try this, start with the basic line-following program. Place the "Light Sensor" icon inside the loop, either before or after the "Switch" icon. You will find this and other sensor icons under the yellow tab in the EV3 software. You will also need a "Display" icon. On the "Display" icon, select "Text". The upper left corner of the "Display" icon will say "Mindstorms" when it is first brought into the

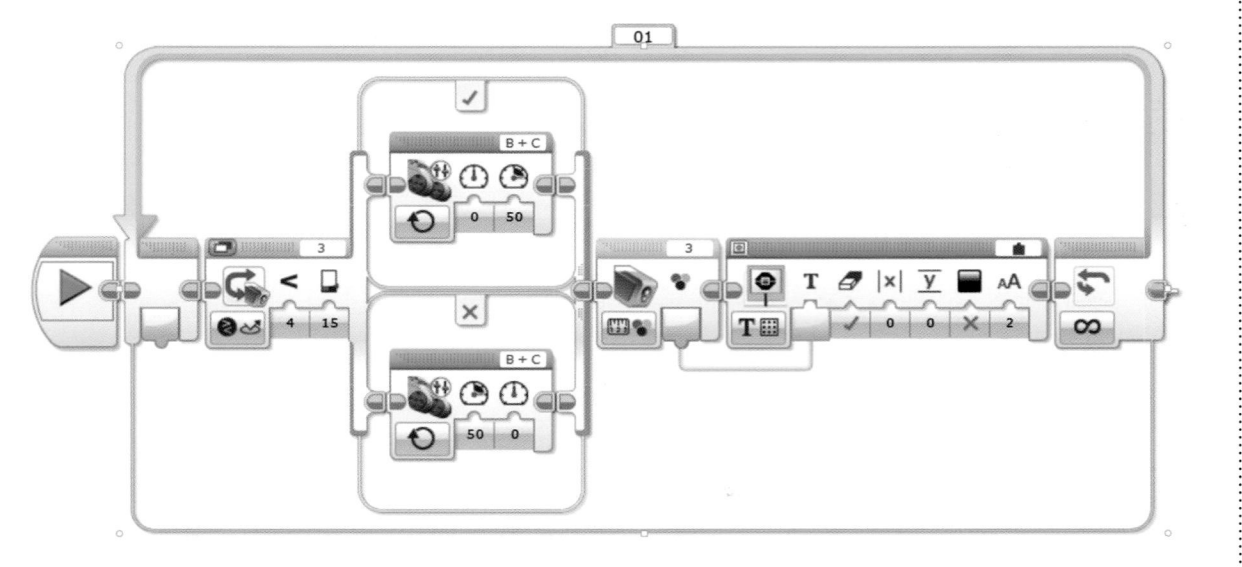

program. Click on that area and select "Wired" instead. Once you have done this, you can pull a yellow "wire" from the "Light Sensor" icon and connect it to the "Display" icon under the "T" tab. On the "Color Sensor" icon, select "Measure–Light Intensity". Remember to set the correct **port** number. When you run the program, you should now be able to see the light values change as your robot moves.

Taking readings from the light sensor is good for more than just troubleshooting. Do you remember making your first line-following program in Level 2? You needed to figure out the exact dark value of the line on your oval and put that information into the

Input and Output

As you work on more advanced programming techniques, you will probably notice that some icons have tabs on the bottom. Those tabs have bumps on either their top or bottom side. If the bump is on the bottom, it means that tab produces an **output**. If the bump is on the top, it means that tab accepts an **input**. For example, the tab on a sensor icon has a bump at the bottom. This is because it can output information to be used by a different icon. The tabs on the "Display" icon are on the top. This means they can accept the information from the sensor icon. To connect an output tab to an input tab, simply click one of them to pull out a yellow "wire" and drag it to the other.

program yourself. Now that you know how to measure values and output them to other icons, you can make your robot do the work for you. Let's program our robot to measure values and use them to follow a line automatically.

Your robot should only read the value once before it begins following the line. This means we need to add some code after the "Start" icon and before the loop. If you put the new code in the loop, the robot would constantly read new values. This is not what we want.

For this program to work correctly, it needs to measure the value from the light sensor and add to it to create the value your robot will use to follow a line. This means you will need to use **variables**. Variables

are values that are stored and used within a program. You can use them to make your program calculate math problems.

Click on the red tab. The first icon in this tab is the "Variable" icon. Pull one of these into your program. In the white space at the top of the icon, you are given the option "Add variable". Select this and type in a variable name. The variable name will help you remember what the number in the variable stands for.

The default setting for a "Variable" icon is "Write Numeric" with a value of 0. When working with variables, it is a good idea to start with a 0 variable before adding other icons. This will ensure that the program is starting from scratch when it begins making calculations.

We want to start our math problem with a measurement value from the light sensor, so add a "Light Sensor" icon from the yellow tab. Add it after the 0 variable icon. Now we want our program to add 5 to whatever value the light sensor reads. Go to the red tab and find the "Math" icon. This is the fifth icon under the tab. It has math symbols on it. Bring it into your program and place it after the "Light Sensor" icon. We want to add, so select the + symbol.

To the right of the + symbol, you will see three tabs on the "Math" icon. They are labeled "a", "b", and "=". The "a" and "b" tabs are for inputs, while "=" is an output tab. Connect a wire from the tab of the "Light Sensor" icon to the "a" tab on the "Math" icon. Now select the "b" tab and type "5". This code will send the value from the "Light Sensor" icon to the "Math" icon, then add 5 to it. This creates a new value.

Now we need to turn the value from the "Math" icon into a variable. Add another "Variable" icon to the right of the "Math" icon. Don't forget to name it the same thing you named the last one. Now use a wire to connect the "=" tab from the "Math" icon to the input tab on the new "Variable" icon.

This program segment will start at 0, read the light sensor, and add 5 to the value of the light sensor reading. It will then put the final value back into a variable. The next step is to use this variable to follow a line.

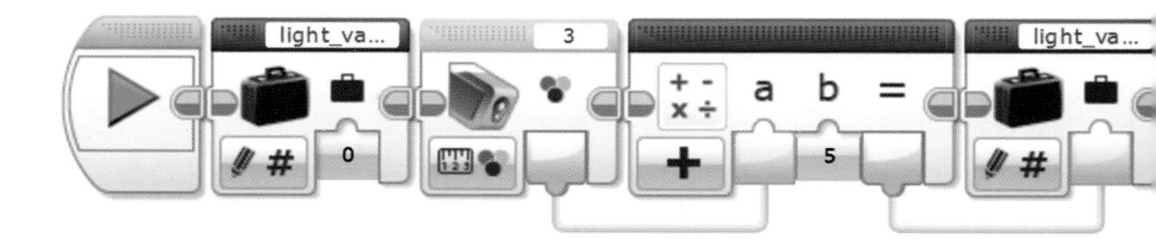

The darker your line is, the easier it will be for your robot to follow.

Look back at the looped part of your line-following program. The "Switch" icon is still set to compare against a value you measured and entered yourself. Instead, we want it to use the value from the variable we just made. Place a new "Variable" icon just inside the loop in front of the "Switch" icon. This time, change the option in the lower left corner of the icon to "Read numeric". Make sure the variable name is the same one you used for the other variable icons in the program. Connect a wire from the new "Variable" icon to the right tab on the "Switch" icon.

You have now created an automatic line-following program. You will not need to read the values from the line yourself. Your program will do it for you! Just make

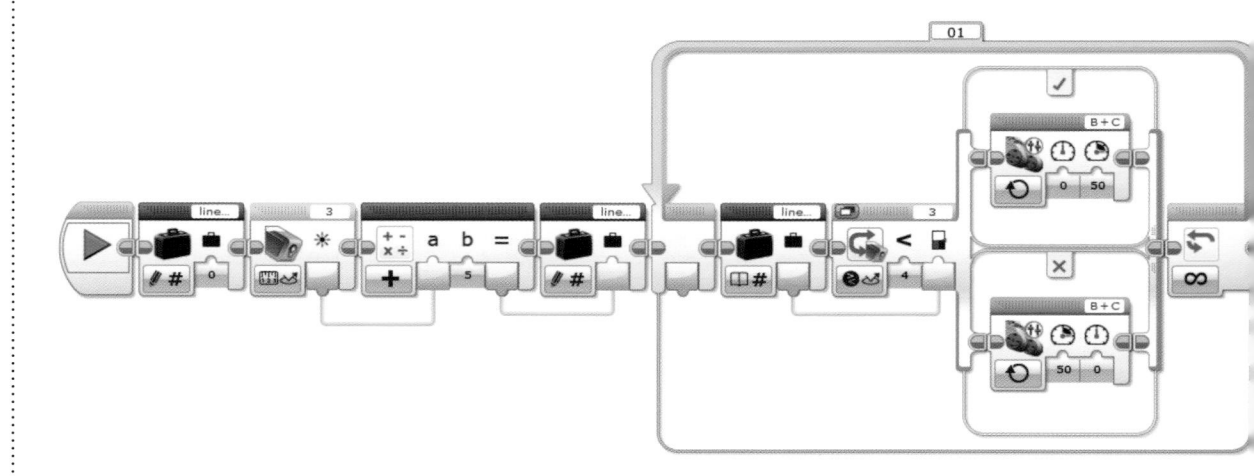

sure the light sensor is on the dark line when you start your robot. Also, remember that this only works if you have a dark line on a light background. What would you need to do if the line is light and the background is dark? There are actually two solutions. You could simply set your robot down to read the dark background instead of the line. The other way is to subtract 5 from your value instead of adding to it.

Chapter 3

Checking a Range

Sometimes when using the ultrasonic sensor, you might want to be within a range of an object rather than checking for a specific distance. For this example, we are going to assume that you want your robot to move until the ultrasonic sensor senses something within 3 to 10 inches (7.6 to 25.4 cm) in front of it. This will be a very simple program that teaches you how to use the range command.

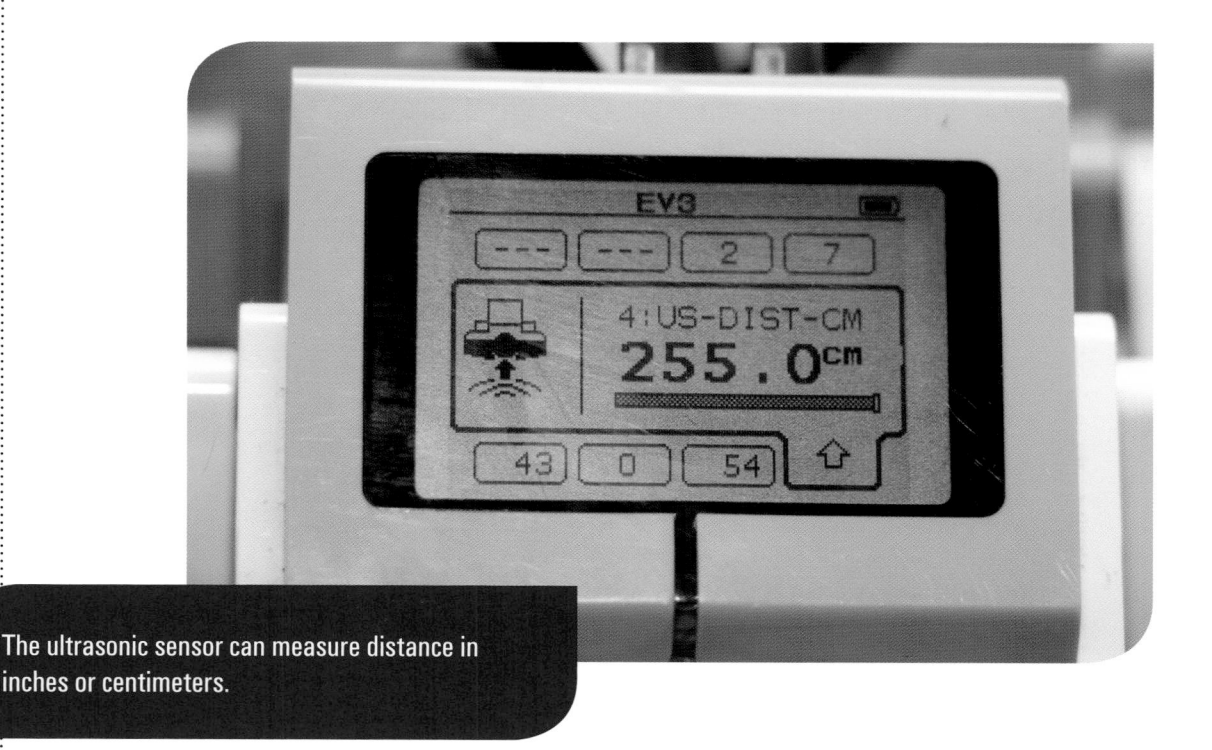

The ultrasonic sensor can measure distance in inches or centimeters.

How the Ultrasonic Sensor Works

Ultrasonic sensors produce sound waves that are outside the hearing range of human beings. These sound waves bounce off objects and return to the sensor. The sensor can then determine how far away the objects are. Ships use similar technology to measure the depth of the ocean and locate other objects underwater. Ultrasonic technology is used for medical purposes, too. For example, it can be used to create an ultrasound image of a baby inside a pregnant mother. It can also be used to diagnose conditions inside the body.

The "Range Command" icon is located under the red tab at the bottom of the screen. You can select either inside of a range or outside of a range by clicking the lower left part of the icon. In this case, you should select inside of a range. There are three tabs to the right of that section. The first tab is the value you will check the range against. The next two values are the limits of your range. To check a range from 3 to 10 inches (7.6 to 25.4 cm), the first tab value should be set to 3 and the second one should be set to 10. So far, though, you have not told it what value you want to check.

Go to the yellow tab and add an "Ultrasonic Sensor" icon to your program. Place it just before

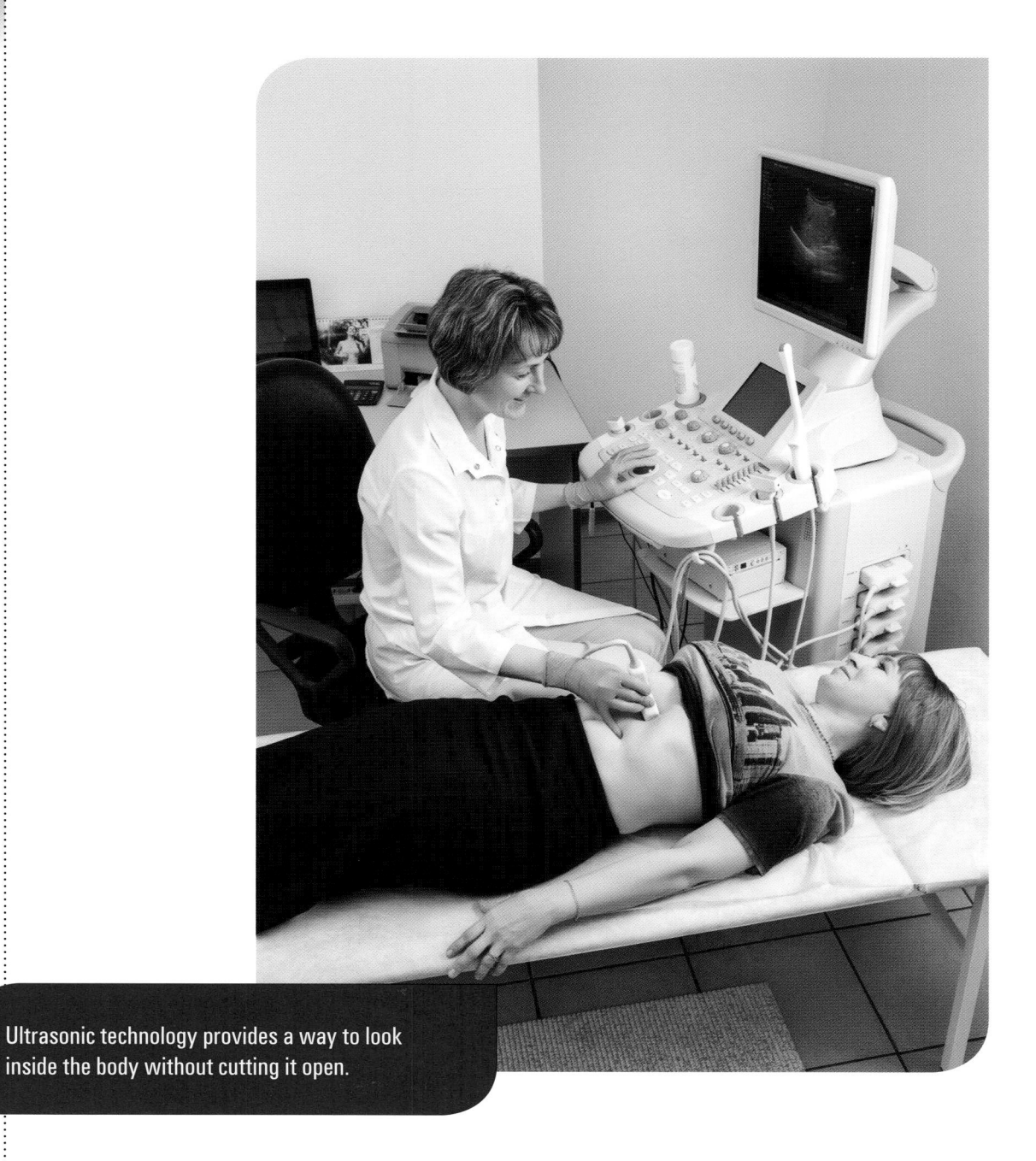

Ultrasonic technology provides a way to look inside the body without cutting it open.

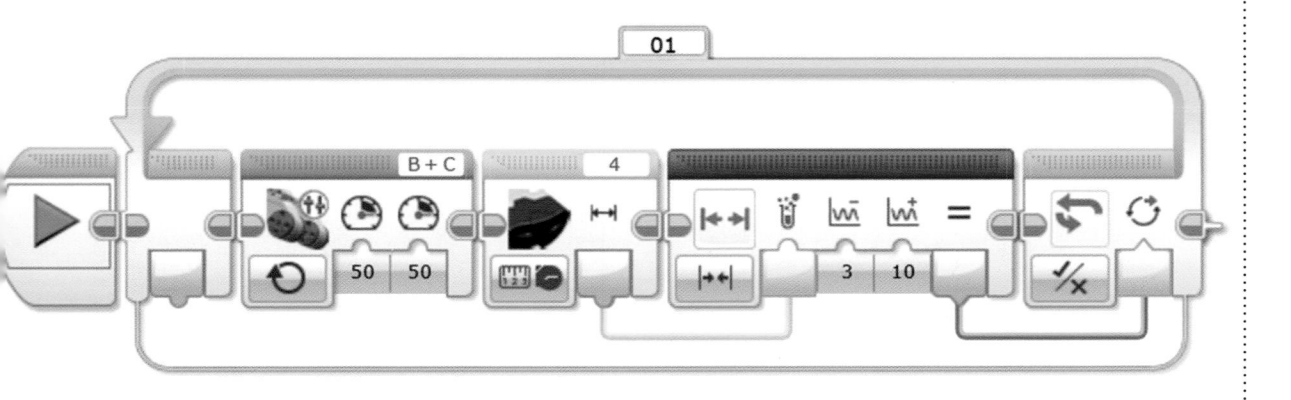

the "Range Command" icon. Set the sensor to measure distance in inches. Now pull a wire from the tab on the sensor icon and connect it to the tab labeled "value" on the range icon. With these two icons connected, your robot will read the value of the sensor and compare it to a range. The next step is to use this result to control something. In this case, you will use it to control a loop. Bring a "Loop" icon into your program and select the "Logic" option from the lower left. Connect a wire from the "=" tab on the range loop to the "until true" tab on the loop. Add a "Move Tank" icon, and you have a program that will

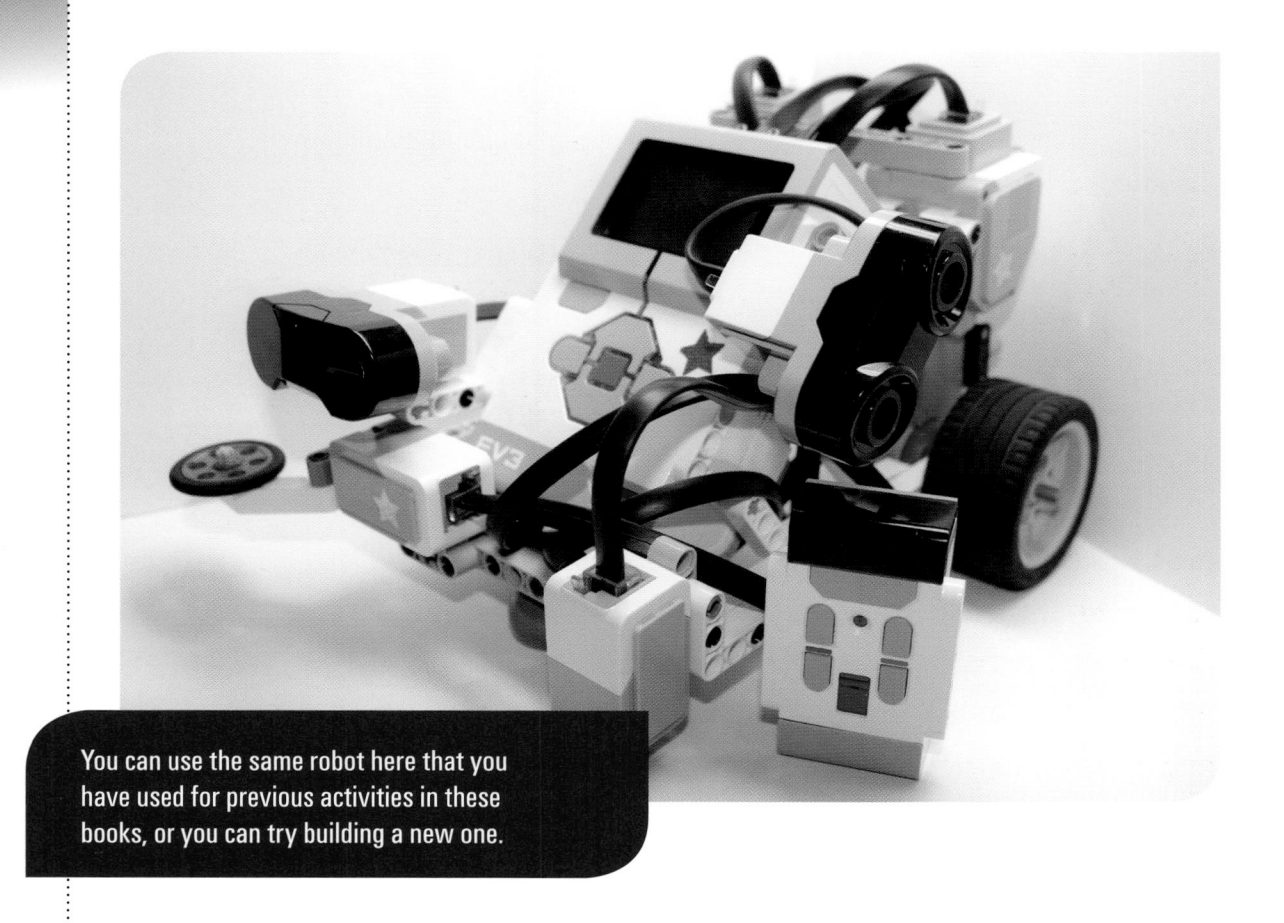

You can use the same robot here that you have used for previous activities in these books, or you can try building a new one.

drive forward until the ultrasonic sensor measures an object that is between 3 and 10 inches (7.6 and 25.4 cm) away.

Chapter 4

Detecting and Counting Lines

There are many interesting applications for the
math icons in the EV3 software. Using the skills
you have learned so far, you should be able to
create a program that can count lines. How do you
think this would work? Which sensors would you use?
Before you read the rest of this chapter, try creating
a line-counting program. Try to make the line count
appear on the display screen of the EV3 unit. Take a
look at the program later in this chapter if you need
some hints. To test your program, use electrical tape
to create some **parallel** lines on a piece of white
poster board. Put different amounts of space between
each line.

Did you get it to work? If not, don't worry. The
program you developed could be correct in theory
but will not work because of the speed of the robot.

When you ran your program, you might have
seen a count that was much larger than the actual

number of lines on your board. When the robot reaches a black line, it reads black just as you would expect. However, the light sensor can read extremely fast. Before the robot gets across the black line, it will read black many times. How do you think you can fix it so it will only count the line once?

There is more than one solution to this problem, but some are better than others. Let's try programming the robot to drive until it sees a line and counts the line, and then drives until it sees white before it starts counting again. This will make sure the robot only counts each black line once.

Start with a "Variable" icon set to 0. Name the variable "Line Count" or anything else that makes sense to you. Just be sure to use the same name for all the variable icons in the program.

Because you only need to set your variable to 0 once, leave this icon outside of a loop. And because your robot is always going to be moving, you can also turn the motors on a single time outside of the loop. The rest of the code should be inside of a loop. For now, you can make it an unlimited loop. Just remember to stop the robot once it has counted all the lines.

The next icon will be "Wait For". Select "Reflected Light" at the bottom left of the icon. Read the line value on your board and make the value here about 5 more. Now place a "Light Sensor" icon. Wire the output from that into the "a" tab of a "Math" icon. Put a "1" in the "b" tab. Be sure the bottom left is set to "add".

Add another "Variable" icon. Now wire the "=" tab on the "Math" icon to the input of the new variable. You also need to connect a second wire from the "=" tab to a "Display" icon. This will cause the total counted lines to appear on the display screen of the EV3. Once everything is in place, load the finished program onto your robot and test it out.

In this book, you have learned how to combine the basic programming skills that you already knew with some more advanced programming techniques. However, there are still many more things you can do

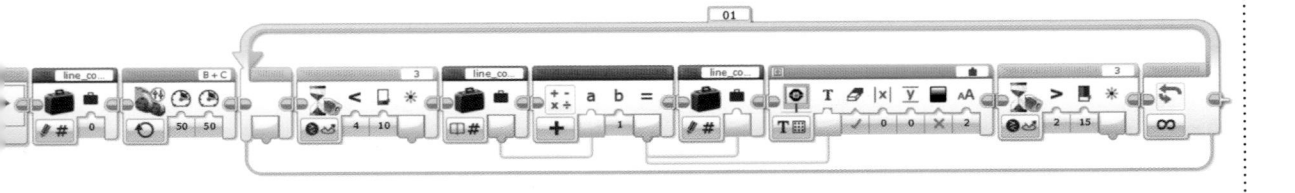

Starting From Zero

Do you remember adding a 0 variable to the start of your program in chapter 2? It is common practice for programmers to zero out all variables before using them, whether they are working with Mindstorms or any other programming language. This ensures that the value of a variable always starts at 0. Some programming languages automatically set variables to 0, but most programmers do not depend on this. The best way is always to set each variable to 0 before using it.

with your EV3. If you're ready for the next step, check out the next book in this series to learn more about some of the educational features of the EV3 and even more advanced programming.

What will you create next?

Glossary

executed (EK-suh-kyoo-tid) carried out a planned action

icons (EYE-kahnz) graphic symbols on a computer screen that represent programs, functions, or files

input (IN-put) information fed into a computer

output (OUT-put) information produced by a computer

parallel (PAR-uh-lel) staying the same distance from each other and never crossing or meeting

port (PORT) place on a computer that is designed for a particular kind of plug

troubleshoot (TRUHB-uhl-shoot) to try different things in an attempt to identify and solve a problem

variables (VAIR-ee-uh-buhlz) symbols that stand for numbers

Find Out More

BOOKS

Garber, Gary. *Instant Lego Mindstorms EV3*. Birmingham, UK: Packt Publishing, 2013.

Isogawa, Yoshihito. *The LEGO MINDSTORMS EV3 Idea Book: 181 Simple Machines and Clever Contraptions*. San Francisco: No Starch Press, 2015.

WEB SITE

Lego Mindstorms: Build a Robot
www.lego.com/en-us/mindstorms/build-a-robot
Check out instructions for building other Mindstorms robots.

Index

"Display" icon, 12–13, 14, 27

EV3 display, 10, 12, 25, 27
EV3 software, 4, 10, 12, 25

firmware, 10

input tabs, 14, 16

light sensor, 13, 14, 15, 16, 19, 26

loops, 7, 8, 9–10, 12, 14, 18, 23, 26

"Math" icon, 15–16, 27
motors, 6, 7, 11, 26
"Move Tank" icon, 6, 7, 11, 23–24

output tabs, 14, 16

"Switch" icon, 8, 9, 12, 18

troubleshooting, 12–13

ultrasonic sensor, 11, 20, 21, 23, 24

values, 9, 12, 13, 14, 15, 16, 18, 19, 21, 23, 27, 28
variables, 14–15, 16, 18, 26, 28

About the Author

Rena Hixon received a bachelor's degree in computer science from the University of Missouri–Rolla (now Missouri University of Science and Technology). She also earned a doctorate in electrical engineering from Wichita State University. She worked as a software design engineer for 11 years and has taught computer science classes at Wichita State for more than 13 years. In 2004, Rena and her husband started a Lego robotics club for homeschooled students. Its aim is to teach engineering principles, emphasizing math and science, to children. Rena has also taught her own Lego robotics camps for 12 years as well as camps at Missouri S&T for several years.

UNOFFICIAL
GUIDES

Did you ever wonder how innovation happens? Or what it takes to turn a new idea into something that works? The Innovation Library takes a look at people and their creative ideas. It explores how lasting contributions are made in diverse fields such as sports, entertainment, medicine, technology, and transportation. Explore the power of being open to different perspectives and sharing failures and successes with others. Discover how acting on creative ideas can lead to new solutions to old problems.

As anyone who is familiar with Mindstorms knows, these robots are more than just toys. They are adaptable and programmable machines that allow users to explore the world of technology. Though there is a lot to learn and discover about Mindstorms, these guides will turn you into an expert in no time.

What will you create?

Read all the titles in the Unofficial Guides series:
MINDSTORMS: Level 1
MINDSTORMS: Level 2
MINDSTORMS: Level 3
MINDSTORMS: Level 4
MINECRAFT Beginner's Guide
MINECRAFT: Enchanting and Potion Brewing
MINECRAFT: Mining and Farming
MINECRAFT: Redstone and Transportation

GR: W
ISBN-13: 978-1634706469

CHERRY LAKE Publishing

OF

UNOFFICIAL GUIDES

Did you ever wonder how innovation happens? Or what it takes to turn a new idea into something that works? The Innovation Library takes a look at people and their creative ideas. It explores how lasting contributions are made in diverse fields such as sports, entertainment, medicine, technology, and transportation. Explore the power of being open to different perspectives and sharing failures and successes with others. Discover how acting on creative ideas can lead to new solutions to old problems.

As anyone who is familiar with Mindstorms knows, these robots are more than just toys. They are adaptable and programmable machines that allow users to explore the world of technology. Though there is a lot to learn and discover about Mindstorms, these guides will turn you into an expert in no time.

What will you create?

Read all the titles in the Unofficial Guides series:
MINDSTORMS: Level 1
MINDSTORMS: Level 2
MINDSTORMS: Level 3
MINDSTORMS: Level 4
MINECRAFT Beginner's Guide
MINECRAFT: Enchanting and Potion Brewing
MINECRAFT: Mining and Farming
MINECRAFT: Redstone and Transportation

GR: T
ISBN-13: 978-1634706452

9 781634 706452

CHERRY LAKE Publishing

KW